TERRORISM CAN BE ELIMINATED: UNRAVELING NOVEL SOLUTIONS

VOLUME 2, ISSUE 1 OF BRILLOPEDIA

ZAKIYYA RASHEED

ISBN 979-888606940-2

Contents

Preface

"Start writing, no matter what. The water does not flow until the faucet is turned on".

-Louis L'Amour

Hundreds of students and professors are contributing their work to Brillopedia, we are here to provide ample information about Law and Contemporary issues. Our aim is to provide a platform for today's generation to express their views and ideas on law and contemporary law.

Publication

This research paper is published in volume 2, issue 1 of Brillopedia

Author

Zakiyya Rasheed

CHAPTER ONE

ABSTRACT

Nations all over the world are attempting to find solutions to terrorism, which is primarily referred to as the violence during peacetime or in a war against non-combatants. Governments pursuing legal measures to tackle terrorism and western powers using warfare to do so have but proved an ineffective solution. Traditional methods of merely condemning terrorist groups, legislating to prevent the inflow of funds to these groups, and more importantly, the US-led warfare on middle east nations to combat terrorism have not only proved inadequate but has also resulted in the large scale killing of innocent civilians. Terrorism is rooted in political problems requiring political solutions. Large scale murder of innocents can never be justified in the name of tackling terrorism. In fact, the so-called terrorists cannot survive without an adequate supply of weapons. 'Where do they get these arms?' is an important question to be deliberated when discussing on terrorism. It is alleged that the United States, being the largest supplier of arms to the third world, and to the Middle East in particular, provides potential terrorists easy access to weapons. Therefore, a more intensive study of the prevailing international legal norms on combating terrorism and effective solutions to extremist violence is absolutely necessary.

This paper includes:

• A comprehensive understanding of the sustenance of terrorism

• The need to step out from the traditional solutions to terrorism that are inadequate

• Proposals to the International Community at large to tackle Terrorism at its very roots

INTRODUCTION

Two types of conflicts constantly take place in the world from time immemorial: The incessant competition for consolidation of power and resources and the struggle for justice. However, the perceptions of different people about conflicts are contrasting.

"One man's terrorist is another man's freedom fighter" is a popular saying. As a matter of fact, either of these two issues can be seen in the demands of the terror groups. All times have indeed seen violent movements against tyrant rules and have been labelled terrorist by the latter. Indian freedom fighters were called anti-nationals by the British. The case of Palestine is also another example of a just freedom struggle being labelled as terrorist by the State of Israel. The struggle for freedom must, therefore, be clearly distinguished from terrorist activities

Another significant issue to be deliberated upon while discussing terrorism is the means used by the terror groups. Resort to violence is universally seen and of course, it is not an acceptable one. While governments possess a plethora of means to suppress such groups, the latter having no access to such means are left with the only option of bargaining by creating terror among the people.

The issue of terrorism must be addressed with a proper understanding of this basic concept. The varying definitions of terrorism reflect the different perceptions. Politics behind the nomenclature is yet another aspect of terrorism. Terrorism, which is rooted in socio-political and economic reasons must be addressed accordingly and be eliminated by eradicating the causes.

CHAPTER THREE

DEFINING TERRORISM

The definition of terrorism will affect communication and response to the issue and so have consequences for society and politics. However, a suitable universal definition seems impractical because different bodies, organisations and government agencies have different definitions to suit their own particular role, purpose or bias.

Walter Laqueur uses the simple, broad definition "terrorism is the illegitimate use of force to achieve a political objective by targeting innocent people". Tore Bjorgo states "terrorism is a set of methods of combat rather than an identifiable ideology or movement and involves premeditated use of violence against (primarily) non-combatants in order to achieve a psychological effect of fear on others than the immediate targets." The US State Department describes terrorism as "premeditated, politically motivated violence perpetrated against non-combatant targets by subnational groups or clandestine agents, usually intended to influence an audience".[1]

The United States and Changing Definitions of Terrorism

International groups labelled 'terrorist' are friends and enemies to world powers. So,'Who and what is real terrorism?' must be defined. Is terrorism the state-sponsored violence by world powers like America and Israel or resistance to that so-called 'War on terror"? The term 'terrorism' came to be used only towards the beginning of the 21st century. Communalism, extremism, fundamentalism, etc. were the phrases used before the advent of 'terrorism'. It is the United States that invented such terminology for their convenience.

Moreover, it is evident that 'world enemies' change according to changes in the US foreign policy. Soviet Russia was a threat to world peace till 1992. America used Afghan Mujahid against USSR. After the collapse of USSR, Muslim countries became the counter pole ofUS. Former friends Afghan

Mujahid was the new threat in 2000. Once Ahmadi Najad's Iran was their enemy; today they have friendly ties with Iran and same is the case with Saddam Hussein.

It can be seen thus that someone's terrorists are freedom fighters for some others.

[1]Gregor Bruce, *Definition of Terrorism – Social and Political Effects*, JMVH (May, 2013), https://jmvh.org/article/definitionof-terrorism-social-and-political-effects/.

CHAPTER FOUR

MYTH V/S REALITY

Interestingly, more people die of road accidents and epidemic diseases than from terrorist attacks across the world. Terrorism is no doubt a problem to be tackled. However, the hype given to it by media and governments, not only helps the terrorists to spread fear but is also futile.

- **Why terrorism persists?**

As aforementioned groups involved in terrorist activities either stand for the consolidation of power and resources or rise against the unjust and unfair governance. So, as long as governments remain arbitrary and blind towards people's needs terrorism shall sustain.

- **Fictional Democracy**

Democracy, commonly said to be the governance by the people though exists in the manifesto of nations around the globe today, is practically non-existent. A major chunk of the population of the so-called democratic countries experiences unfair and autocratic governance. Civil rights and especially the human rights of the oppressed communities are at stake and very often it is these problems that manifest as terrorist activities. Terrorists often justify their acts based on perceived social, economic and political unfairness. Warfare between races, struggles between the rich and poor or battles between political outcasts and elites have been labelled as terrorism.

The 1987 rigging of Kashmir state elections is a good example of a fictional democracy. In 1987, MUF (Muslim United Front) decided to participate in the democratic elections of 1988. MUF was a cluster of all the socio-political and religious organizations who wanted to resolve the dispute by peaceful means. But the Indian government did not allow the movement to flourish. Elections were rigged! Not only that, the government rendered the movement directionless by caging its leaders and activists. Though there was resentment already going on among the people, the rigged election acted as a catalyst. People lost faith in the democratic setup and peaceful process.

- **Political Instability**

Autocratic governments, arbitrary and unjust rule and inequality plays a major role in pushing the oppressed into terrorist groups. The roots of the Syrian civil war for example lie in the Jasmine revolution against the autocratic government.

CHAPTER FIVE

COLONIALISM V/S THE WAR ON TERROR

The empire where the sun never sets ruled the world for years. Colonialism dominated over nations across the world and exploited their natural resources. Today while nations stand independent and free from the shackles of colonial powers, the 'war on terror' has become the new form of colonialism.

America declared the war on terror following the 9/11 attack. While the World tower attack claimed 3000 casualties, America's retaliation killed 10000 innocent civilians by persistent bombings in Afghanistan and the Middle East. Holding Saddam Hussein responsible for the 9/11 attack, America unleashed intensive wars in the Middle East killing thousands of civilians and creating political instability. According to a new study[1], hundreds of thousands of people in Afghanistan, Iraq and Pakistan have been killed due to the so-called "war on terror" launched by the United States in the wake of the September 11, 2001 attack. The report, which was published on 3rd November 2018 by the Brown University's Watson Institute for International and Public Affairs, put the death toll between 480,000 and 507,000. The toll includes civilians, armed fighters, local police and security forces, as well as US and allied troops. Though the American public, press and lawmakers often overlook the war on terror, the increased body count signals that, far from diminishing, this war remains intense.

- **Oil and Natural Resources**

The world witnesses an incessant struggle of the world powers like the United States and Israel to consolidate natural resources. Other nations like Russia and the United Kingdom, etc. support them. These states sponsor terrorism in their rivalry to dominate natural resources as aforementioned. The United States dominates over world resources arbitrarily. Be it oil from Arab countries, gold from African countries, or timber from Latin countries, it is very similar to the old wine, i.e., colonialism.

[1]*US 'war on terror' has killed over half a million people: study*,AL JAZEERA,(November 9, 2018), https://www.aljazeera.com/news/2018/11/wars-terror-killed-million-people-study-181109080620011.html.

CHAPTER SIX

WEAPONS OF MASS DESTRUCTION AND IRAQI INVASION

The best estimates available suggest that more than 250,000 people have died as a result of George W. Bush and Tony Blair's decision to invade Iraq in 2003. A newly released investigative report from the UK government suggests that intelligence officials knew ahead of time that the war would cause massive instability and societal collapse and make the problem of terrorism worse.

In August 2002, Dick Cheney[1] declared, "Simply stated, there's no doubt that Saddam Hussein now has weapons of mass destruction." But as Corn[2] notes, at that time there was "no confirmed intelligence at this point establishing that Saddam had revived a major WMD operation."

[1]*Full text of Dick Cheney's speech*, THE GUARDIAN (2002), https://www.theguardian.com/world/2002/aug/27/usa.iraq.

[2] David Corn et al., *Jeb Bush says his brother was misled into war by faulty intelligence. That's not what happened.*,MOTHER JONES (May 9, 201), https://www.motherjones.com/politics/2015/05/jeb-bush-marco-rubio-iraq-war-intelligence/.

CHAPTER SEVEN

SYRIA: COUNTER-TERRORISM LESSONS

It has been almost seven years since unrest in Syria began and spiralled into a civil war that has killed perhaps 500,000 people and displaced millions more. The war and associated diplomacy offer much to chew on, but the counterterrorism implications are particularly striking—for Syria is both a counterterrorism success and a counterterrorism failure. Syria has witnessed the involvement of state and non-state actors in its civil war: the Syrian government, the United States, Russia, Turkey, Iran, and the rebels. Syrian war offers many lessons for counterterrorism:

1. Civil wars and terrorism go together
2. Enemies are often highly divided
3. Terrorist still rely on state or are aided by them
4. Counterterrorism brings people together, but often only tactically
5. Allies need coordination

Syrian government slams international interference and attacks on its sovereignty, while also accusing the US of war crimes

CHAPTER EIGHT

ARMS EXPORT

Terrorists require weapons to carry out their activities and of course, they are not equipped with the means to manufacture arms on a large scale. 'Where do these groups get the weapons, they require?' is thus an important question to be investigated. In fact, the United States is the largest exporter of weapons. It sold weapons to at least 98 countries between 2013 and 2017 and accounted for 34 percent of global major arms export. Its largest clients were: Saudi Arabia (18% of all sales), UAE (7.4% of all sales), and Australia (6.7% of all sales). On one hand the US vows to combat terrorism and on the other hand, it supplies arms to the so-called terror groups. According to the SIPRI report, 49 percent of all U.S. arms exports went to the Middle East. Spleeters has discovered that the ISIS may have captured the warheads from anti-government militias in the Syrian civil war that had been secretly armed by Saudi Arabia and the United States.[1]

The United States is by far the world's largest dealer of arms, which often fall into the wrong hands. "Quite frankly," says Danny Sjursen, US Army strategist and historian, "the war—selling arms—is one of the last American industries that are left. It's one of the last things the United States does well, that we're still number one at—number one at dealing arms in the world."[2]Research by SIPRI shows that exports by the U.S. accounted for 34% of the major arms exports from 2013 to 2017. Russia was second at 22%. Most of the sales go to what are called "developing nations," which is a pretty broad category that includes all countries except the United States, Russia, European nations, Canada, Japan, Australia, and New Zealand. According to the SIPRI report, America supplied arms to 98 countries, with most of them (49%) going to the Middle East.

With all the arms it is outputting into the world, there have been some alarming examples where America's weapons ended up in the wrong hands. As the U.S. combated the spread of ISIS since 2014, it has increasingly found itself fighting against its own weapons, reported Task and Purpose.[3]

A three-year study published in late 2017 by the arms control group Conflict Armament Research (CAR)[4] saw a clear connection between the weapons of international players and the strength of ISIS. The report says: "*International weapon supplies to factions in the Syrian conflict have significantly augmented the quantity and quality of weapons available to IS forces—in numbers far beyond those that would have been available to the group through battlefield capture alone," stated the report. "These findings are a stark reminder of the contradictions inherent in supplying weapons into armed conflicts in which multiple competing and overlapping non-state armed groups operate."*

Weapon trade, the biggest business in the world, survives through was. It cannot exist in peace. Where there is war, there are weapons. Therefore, it is the vested interest of the world powers engaged in weapon trade that armed conflicts persist in the world. The Rafale Scam is a good example pertaining to the business of weapon trade.

[1] Brian Castner, *Exclusive: Tracing ISIS' Weapons Supply Chain-Back to the US*,WIRED (2018), https://www.wired.com/story/terror-industrial-complex-isis-munitions-supply-chain/.

[2] Charles Koch Foundation,*How America supplies the world with weapons*,BIG THINK (Jul. 31, 2018), https://bigthink.com/charles-koch-foundation/how-america-supplies-the-world-with-weapons.

[3] Jared Keller, *The US Funneled Weapons Into The Fight Against ISIS. They Only Ended Up Making The Militants Stronger,* TASK & PURPOSE(Dec. 14, 2017), https://taskandpurpose.com/isis-weapons-arms-control-report.

[4]*Weapons of the Islamic state*, CONFLICT ARMAMENT RESEARCH (Dec. 2017), http://www.conflictarm.com/reports/weapons-of-the-islamic-state/.

CHAPTER NINE

THE INDIAN CONTEXT

A popular narrative is that terrorism means Kashmir, in India. Terrorism in Kashmir was alleged to be one of the reasons for demonetization! However, the insurgency in Kashmir is a separate matter to be dealt upon. Till date,we have not been able to honour the UN resolution to conduct a plebiscite in Kashmir for self-determination. India has witnessed numerous instances of terrorism. It has claimed lots of lives. But what is alarming is the double standards followed in the conviction of the accused. Communal riots have preceded elections and facilitated vote bank politics. Alleged acts of terrorism have always diverted public interest from major scams. What can be inferred is that terrorism can be a mask to deceive people. It facilitates the activities of the real exploiters in the world. As a matter of fact, Indian political parties have no existence in the absence of Islamic terrorism, Pakistan, and Kashmir. They can divert the real issues. The time, place, and reasons of bomb blasts in India when analysed reflects this reality.

It is an irony that the world's largest democratic country is being ruled by the political outfit of the RSS, the world's largest militant group. This will naturally result in struggles and conflicts within the country. The failure of democracy is the villain here.

- **Mob Lynching**

Mob lynching has become a fashion and passion today in India. There have been 32 cases of attacks by mobs or vigilante groups on Muslims since May 2014[1]. 23 people were killed, including women and children. The pretext of cows was used for committing heinous crimes in most of the cases. Since the present government came to power mob killings of innocent citizens in the name of cow, especially Muslims have increased.

On 17th July 2018, the Supreme Court of India condemned the epidemic of mob lynching and asked the Parliament to draft legislation that would stop people from taking law into their hands. But within hours of the judgement, Swami Agnivesh, a spiritual leader known for promoting communal harmony, was brutally attacked by the members of the youth wing of ruling Bhartiya Janata Party. In an interview with a news agency, CP Singh, a minister of Jharkhand justified the attack saying, "He talks against Hindus, makes anti-national comments, supports Kashmiri separatists and Naxals". C.P. Singh represents the mob that has been given the responsibility of creating a new order in India, where the minority-Muslims, Dalits, and anybody wo speaks on their behalf- are attacked with impunity. Beef ban has been used by these 'terror groups' to justify their attacks on innocent Muslims in public.

Saffron terror is not of recent origin, although its gravity and magnitude have increased since the last 4 years. The 2002 anti-Muslim riots in Gujarat resulted in the death of thousands of Muslims and over 2500 injuries. Though often classified as communal violence, the events of 2002 have been described as a 'pogrom' by many scholars. This genocide serves as the best example of state sponsored terrorism in India.

[1] Subodh Varma, *Cow terrorism killed 23 since 2014*,THE TIMES OF INDIA (Jun. 30, 2017), https://timesofindia.indiatimes.com/india/cow-terrorism-killed-23-since-2014/articleshow/59378467.cms.

CHAPTER TEN

EXISTING INTERNATIONAL AND INDIAN ANTI-TERRORISM LEGISLATIONS

- **UN Global Counter-Terrorism Strategy**

The United Nations General Assembly adopted the Global Counter-Terrorism Strategy on 8 September 2006. The strategy is a unique global instrument to enhance national, regional and international efforts to counter terrorism.

Through its adoption that all Member States have agreed the first time to a common strategic and operational approach to fight terrorism, not only sending a clear message that terrorism is unacceptable in all its forms and manifestation but also resolving to take practical steps individually and collectively to prevent and combat it.

The adoption of the strategy fulfilled the commitment made by world leaders at the 2005 September Summit and builds on many of the elements proposed by the Secretary-General in his 2 May 2006 report, entitled Uniting against Terrorism: Recommendations for a Global Counter-Terrorism Strategy.

- <u>Reviewed every 2 years</u>: The General Assembly reviews the Strategy every two years, making it a living document attuned to Member States' counter-terrorism priorities. The Fifth Review of the United Nations

Global Counter-Terrorism Strategy took place on 1 July 2016. The General Assembly examined the report of the Secretary-General (A/70/826) on the implementation of the UN Global Counter-Terrorism Strategy over the past decade. It also gave further consideration to the Secretary-General's Plan of Action to Prevent Violent Extremism (A/70/674-A/70/675), which was presented by the Secretary-General to the General Assembly in January 2016. The General Assembly adopted the resolution (A/RES/70/291) by consensus.

- <u>Four Pillars</u>: The Global Counter-Terrorism Strategy in the form of a resolution and an annexed Plan of Action (A/RES/60/288) composed of 4 pillars:

1. Addressing the conditions conducive to the spread of terrorism
2. Measures to prevent and combat terrorism
3. Measures to build states' capacity to prevent and combat terrorism and to strengthen the role of the United Nations system in that regard
4. Measures to ensure respect for human rights for all and the rule of law as the fundamental basis for the fight against terrorism.

- **Other International counter-terrorism Conventions**

Today, there are 15 counter-terrorism international conventions in force, which were developed under the auspices of the United Nations and its specialized agencies and the International Atomic Energy Agency (IAEA):

1. Tokyo Convention: Convention on Offences and Certain Other Acts Committed On Board Aircraft (1963)
2. Hague Convention: Convention for the Suppression of Unlawful Seizure of Aircraft (1970)
3. Sabotage Convention or Montreal Convention: Convention for the Suppression of Unlawful Acts Against the Safety of Civil Aviation (1971)
4. Diplomatic Agents Convention: Convention on the Prevention and Punishment of Crimes Against Internationally Protected Persons (1973)
5. Hostages Convention: International Convention against the Taking of Hostages (1979)
6. Nuclear Materials Convention: Convention on the Physical Protection of Nuclear Material (1980)

7. Airport Protocol: Protocol for the Suppression of Unlawful Acts of Violence at Airports Serving International Civil Aviation (1988)
8. Maritime Convention: Convention for the Suppression of Unlawful Acts Against the Safety of Maritime Navigation (1988)
9. Fixed Platform Protocol: Protocol for the Suppression of Unlawful Acts Against the Safety of Fixed Platforms Located on the Continental Shelf (1988)
10. Plastic Explosives Convention: Convention on the Marking of Plastic Explosives for the Purpose of Detection (1991)
11. Terrorist Bombing Convention: International Convention for the Suppression of Terrorist Bombings (1997)
12. Terrorist Financing Convention: International Convention for the Suppression of the Financing of Terrorism (1999)
13. Nuclear Terrorism Convention: International Convention for the Suppression of Acts of Nuclear Terrorism (2005)
14. Beijing Convention: Convention on the Suppression of Unlawful Acts Relating to International Civil Aviation (2010)
15. Beijing Protocol: Protocol Supplementary to the Convention for the Suppression of Unlawful Seizure of Aircraft (2010)

- **Terrorist and Disruptive Activities (Prevention) Act – TADA**

The first anti-terrorism law[1] legislated by the government of India to define and counter-terrorist activities, the Terrorist and Disruptive Activities (Prevention) Act, was in force between 1985 and 1995 under the background of the Punjab insurgency and was applied to the whole of India. TADA led to tens of thousands of politically motivated detentions, torture, and other human rights violations.[2] TADA's pathetic conviction rate of 1 per cent obscured its wide use as a preventive detention measure where more than 76,000 persons were detained for years on end destroying livesand ruining their kith and kin.[3]

- **Prevention of Terrorism Act – POTA**

Passed by the Parliament in 2002, the objective of Prevention of Terrorism Act is the strengthening of anti-terrorism operations. It was repealed in 2004.

S.A.R. Geelani, a lecturer at Delhi University, was sentenced to death by a special POTA court for his alleged role in the 2001 attack on the Indian Parliament. He was later acquitted on appeal by the Delhi High Court on a legal technicality.[4]

[1](The) Terrorist And Disruptive Activities (Prevention) Act,1987, SOUTH ASIA TERRORISM PORTAL, http://www.satp.org/satporgtp/countries/india/document/actandordinances/TADA.HTM#7A (last visited Jan 23, 2019)

[2]Anti-Terrorism Legislation, HUMAN RIGHTS WATCH (2001),https://www.hrw.org/legacy/backgrounder/asia/india-bck1121.htm.

[3]India's Unforgivable Laws, ECONOMIC AND POLITICAL WEEKLY (2018), https://www.epw.in/engage/article/indias-unforgivable-laws?0=ip_login_no_cache=044b862f71453330844d7142273b9533.

[4]Prevention of Terrorism Act, 2002, WIKIPEDIA (2018), https://en.wikipedia.org/wiki/Prevention_of_Terrorism_Act,_2002.

CHAPTER ELEVEN

GOING BEYOND THE TRADITIONAL SOLUTIONS

The problem of terrorism is tackled by governments and international bodies by resorting to aggressive anti-terrorism laws which have proved ineffective. Black laws like the Unlawful Activities Prevention Act, enacted by the government of India, curtail the fundamental rights of citizens and unlawfully detain citizens especially of the minority community for years in jail. But in almost all cases, the detained were acquitted of all charges. Finding apt solutions to a problem lies in the elimination of the root causes of the problem. Terrorism is political violence. Unfortunately, while some political violence is justified, others are said to be unjustifiable and religiously motivated.

To end terrorism as such the socio-political and economic reasons must be removed. The catalysts of terrorism are:

- Poverty
- Inequality
- Injustice
- Unequal representation
- Autocratic governments

To eliminate terrorism completely from the world novel solutions must be undertaken:

- Establish Justice and Fairness
- Ensure employment and a good standard of living
- Ensure proportional representation of all classes of citizens in political power

- Disseminate knowledge
- Curb governmental autocracy and arbitrariness
- Promote value based social order
- Bring about transparent governance
- Establish true democracy
- Complete digitalization
- Abolish monopoly of technology
- A single world army

CHAPTER TWELVE

CONCLUSION

World peace is desired by all. Wars, conflicts, and terrorism are condemned by the common man. Terrorism, being an international crisis to be resolved, is in fact, a threat to world peace. State and non-state actors must collaborate to put an end to terrorism. The international community at large is duty bound to cooperate in all anti-terrorism initiatives. The root cause of terrorism lies in socio-political and economic disadvantage, unfairness, injustice, and inequality. Without addressing these issues, it is impossible to eliminate terrorism from the world. True and just democracy must be established all around the world so that people are not attracted to terrorism or resort to violence. The war on terror and America's military interference in almost all wars of the Middle East have created political instability. The sovereignty of the nations must not be encroached upon.